Richard J Pacey's POETRY/ MUTTERINGS

Collated by Patricia Pacey

MAPLE
PUBLISHERS

Richard J Pacey's Poetry / Mutterings

Author: Richard J. Pacey†

Collated by Patricia Pacey

Copyright © 2025 Patricia Pacey

The right of Patricia Pacey to be identified as author of this work has been asserted by the author in accordance with section 77 and 78 of the Copyright, Designs and Patents Act 1988.

First Published in 2025

ISBN 978-1-83538-525-8 (Paperback)
   978-1-83538-526-5 (E-Book)

Book Cover Design and Layout by:
   White Magic Studios
   www.whitemagicstudios.co.uk

Published by:
   Maple Publishers
   Fairbourne Drive, Atterbury,
   Milton Keynes,
   MK10 9RG, UK
   www.maplepublishers.com

A CIP catalogue record for this title is available from the British Library.

All rights reserved. No part of this book may be reproduced or translated in any form or by any means, electronic or mechanical, including photocopying, recording or by any information storage and retrieval system without written permission from the author.

The views expressed in this work are solely those of the author and do not reflect the opinions of Publishers, and the Publisher hereby disclaims any responsibility for them. This book should not be used as a substitute for the advice of a competent authority, admitted or authorized to advise on the subjects covered.

CONTENTS

LISTEN	1
LIQUID INSPIRATION! OR I'M PUZZLED!	2
TATE-STI	3
LONG	4
CAMPAIGN/PARTLY POLITICAL BROADCAST	5
THE STRENGTH OF SONG	6
FUTURUS SUM	7
UNTITLED	8
UNTITLED	9
OUR MEMORY OBEYS IN ???????? LIES.	10
UNTITLED	12
UNTITLED	14
A CHALLENGE	15
ENTRANCE	16
UNTITLED	17
ABANDONED HOPE	18
THE LIVING WORLD	21
THE PRISONER	23
A DEDICATION	24

SATURDAY	25
ON VICTORY	27
CONFUSION, OPPRESSION AND THE RIGHT TO BE FREE	28
APPROACHING THE CITY BY NIGHT	30
DISCO-DANCE DISEASE	32
UNTITLED	36
VAMPIRES	37
WITHIN WITHOUT	39
SOLILOQUY	40
NEW DEPARTURES/NEW BEGINNINGS	41
SEMPRE SI?	43
FLAME	44
CIRCE	45
REMEMBRANCE	46
FANATICS (1)	47
(UN) REALISATION	49
UNTITLED	51
UNTITLED	52
HEUTE, DIE WELT - MORGEN...?	54
WITH AGE COMES	55
THE GRASS IS GREENER	57

OLD KRAKOW	58
DEVOTION	60
TOGETHERNESS	61
UNTITLED	62
TIME AND (E) MOTION	63
REVELS OF BACCHUS	65
UNTITLED	66
BEYOND	67
ABOVE	68
A SONG FOR EUROPE	69
EDITIONS OF YOU	71
2HB	73
JUST ANOTHER HIGH	75
CAN'T LET GO	77
UNTITLED	81
ALISON	83
UNTITLED	84
SENIOR CITIZENS	87
YOURS SINCERELY	88
A CHALLENGE	89
ITALIAN CLUBS – GOOD AND BAD	90

INSPIRATION	91
SAVE	92
WEAKNESS	93
LOOKING FORWARD TO SILVER (HI-HO)	94
KATIE'S POEM	96
CLOSURE	97
PISS TROUGH	98
NOT A GARDENING IMPLEMENT (IN THE VERNACULAR)	99
RE-WRITE	100
STREAMS OF CONSCIOUSNESS, RIVERS OF THOUGHT	101
WHY BOTHER?	102
MUSIC	103
THIS	104
PROFIT AND LOSS	105
DRIPPING TAPS	106
1-O (MEDITERRANEAN SET)	107
SMILE	108
ASPIRATION FOR MANKIND	109
FEELING DOWN?	110
COW - WATCHING FOR BEGINNERS	111
ON FELINES	112

RAINBOW GIRL	114
THE EX-RAINBOW.	116
SELF TAUGHT (TAUT-OLOGY)	118
FISH	119
HALF - EMPTY BED.	121
VOICES	123
WHAT CALMS YOU DOWN?	125
THE GIG RACE	126
FINE NIGHT OUT.	130
UNTITLED	132
OVERHEARD CONVERSATION AT DAN LOWRY'S	133
ALISON	135
GIBBONS	136
THE GREAT VILE SHIFT	137
ARTIST'S PORTRAIT OF A YOUNG MAN	139
DECK OF CARDS	140
AUTUMNAL EDEN	141
UNTITLED	142
UNTITLED	143
£39,95(O!)	145
UNTITLED	146

UNTITLED	147
UNTITLED	148
UNTITLED	149
UNTITLED	151
SEAMUS	152
UNTITLED	153
UNTITLED	154
UNTITLED	156
UNTITLED	157
PORTRAIT OF THE ARTIST	158
KATRINA	159
FREYJA	160
UNTITLED	161
UNTITLED	162
SPOT THE DON - A PROLOGUE	163
UNTITLED	165
SPOT THE DOG III	167
BUCKFASTLEIGH - QUIET QUAINT,	172
ASHBURTON	173
YEALMPTON	176
ORESTON	177

TUESDAY	179
ST. AUBYN - WARM WELCOME.	185
MOUNT EDGCUMBE MASONIC HALL —	187
WED. KING'S ARMS, ORESTON–	189
BUCKFASTLEIGH –	193
SPOT THE SPROG (DOG II THE SEQUEL)	198
ALEXANDRA	201
IDLE POESY	202

LISTEN

The random chairs
Appear everywhere,
Inviting us to sit and ponder,
Knowledge,
Passion,
The inner wonder

Feelings left
Upon the shelf,
Dust encrusted
Upon the heart

Open up,
Ignore the stares
Listen to
The random chairs.

Poland / E-Berlin
Burning Stars

LIQUID INSPIRATION! OR I'M PUZZLED!

What is this synchronicity,
That exists between a beer and me?
That gives me words
That makes you think?
I wonder,
Ponder,
Gesture yonder,
Perhaps I'll have another drink…

TATE-STI

As in Tate Lyle- sugar for
Your "tea" from the kettle
And wink...

Does she sing, does she dance,
Does she drink?
You hope to have a ghost of a chance,
After all, it's been a while,
A casual glance,
And when you catch her smile,

Whether you claim to have been
Sailing or rowing
When you see a damsel in distress

It's all about knowing
Which buttons to press.

A LEARNING PROCESS.
Let's process and proceed
In the hope we might succeed together.

LONG

Passing you by is such suffering, soul,
Full of light and darkness combined,
When I think of you reflected.
Longings echoing in my mind,
Are all that I hear,
Be near.

Now, wasted moments in ponder
In the solitude of thought
Glazed impressions staring out at me,
All I ever saw in you is fraught,
With all that I hear,
Be near.

Inspirations of past recollections wind
In the reaches of shadows late,
Your vision surrounding me still
Through the pain, but I'm potent, I still wait,
For all that I hear,
Be near.

In short I long.

CAMPAIGN/PARTLY POLITICAL BROADCAST

Flames consuming
Passion destroying
Everything safe
But no sound.
They march as it burns,
Down the roads
Wide and long,
Singing the party faithful's song.
The life they preach
They destroy on their route
Never questioning,
Safe in the knowledge
That no-one can teach.
Their twisted notions of life and faith.
Live in emptiness,
Souls abandoned, they never rest,
Hearts encancered
With the hatred that they love best.

THE STRENGTH OF SONG

The rhythm and rhyme which
The people consume,
Forms the basis of our society,
But the life which is contained therein,
Will finally set the people free.

Mindless movement nurtures thought
Hazy though it be,
But only the movement within the mind
Enables us to see.

When all the music comes to one,
Harmonious, powerful, spirited song,
Then all the world shall be as one,
And then we shall be free.

FUTURUS SUM

As time slipped by
The chorus grey,
The siren's voice decried,
The marble prophecy of
ending day,
The living flame belied,
Where mortal fears
Succumb to woe,
And petrifaction reigns,
This hell-on-earth where
all must go.
For ever rapt
In self-made chains.

UNTITLED

You stood tall,
But wavered, as a sapling
in the breeze,
Shining, living, breathing,
Such vitality,
Such great beauty,
Finally wavering,
Fighting to breathe on still.
Your own sweet scent
Is dulled by death,
Best your memory
Lingers on.

UNTITLED

It was dark when I awoke last time
The silence echoed out,
While the world slept on I sought escape
But only the walls laughed back
The chorus sing, the memories flood,
Musical souls entwine
But all the tastes of life and love
Are shades in the abstract mind
I raced through reason
Tore through slate,
A crimson stain on snow white dreams
As life and love collide in hate,
The door still blocked my living screams

OUR MEMORY OBEYS IN ???????? LIES.

Dark, and midnight
Black, the windows
To a world of light

River flowing, gleaming
Cascade, celebration
Of a world of life

Becoming, inviting, full
Of rose-red beauty
And the joy of life.

Enchanters beguiling
With whispers and promise
Of the worth of the world
In a life shared with thee.

O, Inspiring Muse,
Hear my plea,
Hear my dedication
To thy beauty and thy grace,

Thy essence,
Without which I,
Merely mortal,
Can only ever merely exist
Inspire me, o wondrous Muse,
That I may live,
Which is the light thyself.
Make me whole,
Make me
One with thee.

UNTITLED

There is a place called Ridgeway,
Near Gorse Hill, in Swindon,
And it's been the ruin of many a poor boy,
And God, I know, I'm one.

I grew up on the radio,
In the days of legacy
And now we're on the UCAD,
Oh Lordy, please help me
Now the only thing I do all day,
Is count up my alerts,
And that explains the reason why,
My head, it always hurts.

Got one hand on my mouse pad,
The other holds a drink,
This patch can drive you crazy,
If you could stop to think.

Oh, mother, tell your children,
Not to do what I have done,
Come out of your training,

And go live on day one.
When the day, is young.
And the UCAD goes mad,
And alerts, are the only.
we'll see,
No. I won't be afraid,
No I won't shed a tear,
Just as long,
As you stand.
Stand by me.

Hotel UCAD inform
On a dark desert highway.

You Never closed your eyes.
When you touched your mouse
with your fingertips,
Now there's no relevance,
Anymore.
In why you do just this.
You've got that UCAD feeling
Wooah that UCAD feeling
You've got that UCAD feeling
Now it's gone, gone, gone,
Whooo-ooo-ah.

UNTITLED

Copper flocked eyes gleam,
A barrier more subtle than language.
Steely purpose radiates,
Spokes without a wheel
Silence numbs the heart,
A blanket of smothering guilt.
Elemental guise and grief,
Her poise and posture
Cannot save her.

For every copper coin,
There is vert-de-gris,
For every steel span,
There is rust,
Crystal shimmers,
Then it shatters,
Even elements cannot resist
The elements,
Struts and raves
Become stutter and graves,

A CHALLENGE

I believe in her,
In everything she does,
Do my eyes deceive me?
Does my mind deceive my eyes?
As I think of the way,
That she makes my life complete.
I shudder within,
Is this dependency?
Like a drug she penetrates.
With needle-sharp ecstasy,
And I will not hear.
A word,
Against her,
I feel everything.
So I believe in her.
I must,
But does she
Believe in me?

Gorizia-N.E. Italy
18/04/92

ENTRANCE

Her entrance and her smile
Raise such confused feelings,
That I hardly know why or how
I am
Anymore.
For better or for worse
These glances exchanged,
May mean different things,
For there is always a differing
Of mind and emotion
A way
Of life.
Whose?
Gorizia-N.E. Italy
18/04/92

UNTITLED

I walked the long and lonely road,
Towards the summit of my dreams,
Yet the path is veiled and the
Bridge to cross,
Is ever growing longer ahead.

As I move on forward to my distant goal,
I sense the spirit's far flung cage,
Yet soon my hope will fully awaken,
Bringing my genuine life back to life.

I feel as I walk through the streets
At night,
Shades of my reality,
Yet still I am unable to discover,
The real reality of the truth of my being.

29 JUNE, 1991

ABANDONED HOPE

It was dark when I awoke last time.
The silence echoed out:
While the world slept on I sought escape,
But only the walls laughed back,
Decay grabbed hold as I caught my breath,
Shades of shades in the abstract mind.
And once I die, relief I'll find.

The chorus sing,
The memories flood,
Realisation binds,
And all the tastes of life and love
Are shades in the abstract mind.

A kiss of blood on sun-bleached anger,
A dearth of time swung over me,
Conflicting tastes of flight and dogma,
Where the pleading force abound:
I fled inside to greater spaces,
Voices smiled at my disgrace,
Tried to hide in hidden faces.
Supine forms with ardour laced.

The chorus sing,
The memories flood,
Realisation binds,
And all the tastes of life and Love
Are shades in the abstract mind.

As time slid by the chorus gray,
The siren's voice decried,
My memory fades in sepia lies,
Fleece blown graves with unarmed flaws,
Reams of image beckoned me,
Onyx sores on a scarlet field,
I sang across a drowning sea,
Frosted pains in turns concealed.

The chorus sing,
The memories flood.
Realisation binds:
And all the tastes of life and love
Are shades in the abstract mind.

Specifics writhed when sleep awoke.
The crack glowed bitter sweet in stone,

A pale stigmata of weeping joy.
Overcame my bone-stripped mind,
I raced through reason, tore through slate.
A crimson stain on snow-white dreams,
As life and love collide in hate,
The door still blocked my living screams.

THE LIVING WORLD

(OR THE SHAPE OF THINGS TO COME)

Here I sit,
Thinking thoughts of time-spun colour,
Woven into opaque words,
As human life is ever duller,
People flock in mindless herds.

I look around,
The tangled metal shrieks and falls,
Past triumphs dead and dying,
The neophyte the greenbelt mauls,
Whilst nature looks on, crying.

My heart recoils,
Smell the bland stench of misgiving,
Not a spark of hope remains,
For the wasted masses living,
Fettered in their self-made chains.

I reach out,

Groping for an intact ideal,
Pure in a corrupted world,
Where men from one another steal,
Fighting under banners furled.

Tastes assault me,
Bitter as existence dreary,
Purposes destructive all,
All their minds grow ever weary,
Into darkness they shall fall.

My ears ring,
With a cacaphony of sound,
Wailing from a thousand hearts,
Of hopeless people all around,
Here all will end but nothing starts.

THE PRISONER

OR
CHILDREN'S GAMES

It is ten o'clock at night,
When the escape begins,
The sirens wail in vengeful rain,
The prisoner breaks the hinge.

Engines roar in fast pursuit,
The escapee flees down slopes,
Heading on a northern route,
Recapture kills his hopes.

Curfew silences his cell,
His motivation dies,
In his own solitary hell,
He lies alone and cries.

A DEDICATION

What dim secrets lurk
Behind your eyes of ice?
What deceptions are masked
By your apparent sincerity?
How am I to tell?

Is the pain you feel a reality
Or just another well-planned facade?
And is your love as pure as I see it to be
Or just a vision, painted with eloquent words?
How am I to reason fact
From the fiction you project?

Your see-through schemes of vicious scorn,
Unthinking means of mental torture,
Wrack me, deep inside I'm torn,
With love or hate for thee.

SATURDAY

At night he moves, ever in hope
Of a common, elusive prize,
Searching through the clouds of smoke,
With alcohol reddened eyes.

Time draws in on the disco floors,
As he gives a frantic glance,
Over the embracing, passionate hordes,
For a free girl who might want to dance.

A couple more drinks deaden the pain
Of a seemingly worthless night out,
When sudden perception enters his brain,
And his weary heart raises a shout.

With effort to walk in his stupor self-made,
He approaches the girl with a smile.
Aspirations renewed which had started to fade,
As they sit there and talk for a while.

The last song is played and numbers exchanged,
'Twixt the couple which lust doth surround,
She smiles at the thought of the meeting arranged,
And he at the trophy he's found'.

ON VICTORY

A surge of emotion poured through my body,
My mind elated lie the hero of old,
Agamemnon and Odysseus in their glorious palaces,
Undefeated by laconic demeanour,
With the resolve of Jason I stood against the challenge,
And overcame the taunting voice of long-dead failures,
The strength of Heracles came to me then,
Formed into the determination to prevail,
As Theseus I explored the mazes of my mind,
Unravelling the trail to success and perseverance,
With Perseus in mind I looked my fears in the face,
And defeated the petrifying cynicism of self-doubt,
And then as Bellerophon I reached my Olympus,
Mounted on the winged horse of realised dreams.

CONFUSION, OPPRESSION AND THE RIGHT TO BE FREE

Tension binds my body
Confliction rules my heart
Pressure lies within me
It's tearing me apart.
It's evil and relentless
In its one and only aim
To render my submission
To this foul unholy game.
Black and white do not exist
Everything is grey,
My mind, my life, my being
A state of disarray.

Independence once so great
Identity has gone.
I can't ignore the loaded guns
The stage I am upon.
Each decision, every choice
Does not affect just me
It changes people, alters things
The images they see

Solitude I seem to seek
Freedom at the least
But then I will have nobody
To share my stolen feast.
In this world of luxury
No one seems to care
For all the things that matter most
What's love, what's hate, what's fair.

So here I lie all by myself
Chaos, but no shame
For I am me, the only one
Accountable for blame,
Darkness screens and stillness shouts
The shadows start to moan
My racing heart, my jumbled mind
Say 'Just leave me alone.'

[7/9/89]

APPROACHING THE CITY BY NIGHT

Sixty miles from London and the coach stops once more. An inn. The Red Dragon shines with transplendent luminescence as a multitude of ostlers pour out of the doorway to change the horses, as the postillion draws them to a halt. A young man, resplendent in the uniform of a captain in the king's navy ascends the steps to the post chaise and seconds later the postillion cracks the whip and the coach continues on its journey.

Penetrating the Stygian darkness the horses accelerate as if trying to escape from an unseen pursuer. The naval officer sits, sour faced, pondering over a lost battle or a deceased relative. Malformed trees overhang the roadway like malevolent vultures, reaching out emaciated digits, ready to snatch up their prey, ripe for the picking.

Thirty miles and a change of horses later the carriage stops for the toll bridge. The gate keeper stretches out his arm, his gaunt face tired yet gleeful in anticipation of money , like a dog salivating over the thought of a bone. The officer reaches into his pockets and takes out a shilling, grossly overtipping the beaming man with apparent lack of care. A slight creak breaks the death like silence as the gates open and the coach continues.

Faint sounds of chimes from a distant church clock ring out the witching hour of midnight as the horses strain to drag the cumbersome vehicle up, the first in a long series of hills. The moon, altar of the lupine lords, rests like a pearl on black velvet high above, unchanged but everchanging. Cries of the postillion ring out through the impenetrable Cimmerian blackness as he dismounts to push the post chaise up the steep gradient. The brow of the hill is finally reached and the coachman clambers back aboard.

About five miles in the distant countryside a yellow tinted glow surrounds an immense mass of dark structures: London. The white mares change positions to ease their strain and with the clatter of wheels on a stony road and the sharp bite of the whip on horse flesh the coachman starts the coach moving, the horses galloping with renewed vigour.

The glow of light expands and outlines the seething mass of early morning traffic as night withdraws its dark clutches and the sun brings a watery, shimmering brightness to the world. The post chaise draws to a final halt and the naval officer leaves the carriage and strides off through the dirt infested streets.

21st March, 1986

DISCO-DANCE DISEASE

Now coloured lights are flashing,
Down upon the dancing floor,
And there's just not enough boys,
Coming through the door.
There's rumours in the entranceway.
And anger in the hall.
Somebody laughed at Pawley,
'Cause he was so small,
There's a seekin' in the corner.
They're tryin' to find a chair.
There's a leakin' in the washroom,
There's a sneakin' everywhere.
Somewhere in the corridor someone was heard to sneeze,
Goodness me, goodness me, it's Disco-Dance Disease!
The old D.J. was crucified for staying in the room.
Making music deafening,
And singing out of tune,
Pupil or teacher, they're all down on their knees,
Praying that they won't all get the Disco-Dance Disease,
There's panic on the drinks stand,
Trouble in the loo,

'Cause the new D.J. is playing nothing new,
Some blame the door-staff,
Some the employees,
Everybody knows that it's the Disco-Dance Disease,

Yeah, now the dancers are disgusted,
The D. J. is warped,
The music is too loud,
For anyone to talk,
Everyone seeks damages,
Everyone agrees.
That these are classic symptoms of a lack of new L.P.'s,
At D.H.S. and Notre Dame,
They talk about the curse,
Philosophy is useless,
Reality is worse,
Sophie's just got Ruxpin in a really nice tight squeeze,
Whilst Hutchins invents words that mean:
Disco-Dance…
Disease.

Andrew Laurillard declares:
"I'm not surprised to see you here,
You've got dancer's limp from dancing,
And you're broke 'cause Coke's too dear,
I don't know how you came to get that mark upon your jeans,
But worst of all, young man, you've got the Disco-Dance Disease,"
He wrote out a prescription,
He said, "I am depressed,
Because the girls that Pacey's got are by far the best,
Come back and see me later, next 3rd Year please,
Send me another victim of the Disco-Dance Disease."

I go down to Plymouth Albion,
I'm-a-thunderstruck,
They got dancing Tysoes,
Ruxpin's in luck,
Two girls say they're Heather,
One of them must be wrong,
There's a Daniel Pawley,
He's singing a protest song.
He says "I cannot get a girl,

I can't get one at all,
I cannot get a girl,
'Cause I am much too small,
I cannot get a girl 'cause I can't see above her knees,
I cannot get a girl 'cause I've got Disco-Dance Disease!"
They want to put the lights on,
To make you all go blind,
They put music on full volume,
And try to blow your mind,
Gimme a telephone number,
Hope to see you all next week,
And hopefully by then Tysoe will not be so meek,
Meanwhile, the first Heather says "I'll see you soon,
Perhaps tomorrow morning or Friday afternoon."
The other one's out on hunger-strike,
Her guide dog's got the fleas,
Even Heather's got the Disco-Dance Disease.

UNTITLED

In a cold and darkened Reading light,
A ray strikes out, a gleaming light,
Holding promise of warmth and cheer,
With a wide selection of excellent beer.
Good company is guaranteed,
An honest crowd in thought and deed,
For weary folk requiring rest
And relaxation, they're the best.
All tensions here you may release,
For fun and games, they never cease,
This Broad Street haven from the storm
Of daily life is even warm.
This is the place
The London Tow Campaign anon!

VAMPIRES

Gradually infect people -- not necessarily evil but not natural.

Hero - young but cynical, black-eyed, World weary but nevertheless noble, sacrifices himself to vampires to rave girl/woman he loves.

Does not realise he loves her – indeed rather fears her: she herself recently became a vampire with most of his friends.

Vamps divided though -- not all evil some good but merely rebellious -- his girl and friends in last category although one or two in joint category.

Evil attacks good – driving them out

Hero still only human and weak compared to full vamps, who nevertheless cannot expose themselves in front of his friends.

Hero = History Teacher

Sit = Alien whips / watch – towed tripods over every major town (?) on earth.

Keep peace

Hero hates oppression of aliens, comparing to Nazis etc.

Teaches of how aliens stopped

WWII – atom bombs on New York, Manchester Kier, Hiroshima, Leipzig etc.

Discovers towers empty, aliens dead years ago – compares to Hewells tripod aliens.

Tells all they are free,
Violence begins,
He creates what he has done,
the end.

WITHIN WITHOUT

Love is for fools
And married couples,
A coupling is far
From the romantic ideal,
Ideals are far from me.

This cold-hearted feeling
Is all that protects me,
ALL that supports me,
Against the world,
Invulnerable.

Possibly one day things will be different,
Possibly one day things will be pure,
For the moment the cancer
Of self-degradation,
Is all that is sure.

Gorizia-N.E. Italy
18/04/92

SOLILOQUY

To use or to be used,
That is deception.
Whether 'tis colder in hind-sight,
To succour the barbs and daggers
Of outreaching spite,
Or to suffer the harm
Of drowning frigidity,
And by accepting
End it.
Aye, there lies death.

Gorizia-N.E. Italy
18/04/92

NEW DEPARTURES/NEW BEGINNINGS

After time a native land
Fades, is no longer quite as native
As before, as the natives have been,
Other lands are there to partake in,
Join the way of the wanderer,
Remain as long as you may
But all must move on,
Sometime,
More of it is what is needed,
That is all that we do not have,
But what we must try and find,
Time enough for new beginnings,
Time enough for life,
For laughter,
For love.
All must move on,
Sooner or later,
But a part of me will always be here,

Laughing
and loving
And living.

Gorizia-N.E. Italy
18/04/92

SEMPRE SI?

Whether it be drinks or food,
Never turn it down.
In the hotel bar
They left food out,
We took it,
We ate it,
They poured us beer,
We took it,
We drank it.
There were women too,
We looked.
But did not touch,
Some nights food and drink
Are just enough.

Gorizia-N.E. Italy
18/04/92

FLAME

You stand tall,
But waver,
A sapling in the breeze,
Shimmering, shining,
Coursing, consuming,
Vital, beautiful,
Living.

Finally faltering,
Fighting for breath,
Your own sweet light
Is dulled by death,
Fatally flickering,
Fading away,
Your memory lingers on.

08/12/95

CIRCE

Deep and midnight eyes,
Dark, the windows
To a world of light.

Spirit flowing in gleaming cascade,
In high celebration
Of a world of light.

Becoming, inviting, full,
Rose-red beauty, promising joy
In a world of light.

Enchantress beguiling,
With whispers and motions,
Bring me the pleasures
Of your light-filled world.

08/12/95

REMEMBRANCE

Panic clutches at her heart,
Terror, tearing, thought consuming,
Broken-minded, doubt it whispers,
Tearful sorrow now embraces.

Gone, the warmth of tender loving,
Gone, the reason for her living,
Past, the cares of old romance,
Lying like a shattered dream.

Bittersweet the memory of him,
Bringing pain to heart and soul,
Empty voices calling to her,
Simply murmurs on the wind.

Desperation takes the foreground,
Clutching for a spark of comfort,
Any hope to ease her loss,
Any hope is lost.

25/11/95

FANATICS (1)

They sing as they march
In a passionate throng,
Chanting the party faithful's song,
Blind in their purpose,
Deaf to the sound,
Of the screams of the people,
They cast to the ground.

Theirs is the only way,
Theirs is the best,
Follow my Leader
And death to the rest,
Resistance is futile,
Progress the word,
Today the country,
Tomorrow the world!

The Leader will stop it,
The rot, the decay,
Restore the lost glory
And bring the new day,
As blindly they follow,

Like sheep to the block,
They build their own prison
And inside are locked.

08/12/95

(UN) REALISATION

Twisted shades of reds and blues,
Forming in my mind's dark eye,
To shape tomorrow's ghostly hues,
The future as it sighs.

Midnight's sorrow grapples fast,
Clutching thoughts and asking "why?"
Is time-aged hope all that stands fast?
Yesterday ever wise?

Golden dawn untangles now,
Bringing colour as I die,
And peace that forces me to bow,
My head towards life's lies.

Chords of sweet harmony,
Cut across the discord,
That comes with daily feeling,
Bringing fresh thought,
And notion of what may be.

Chords of sweet disharmony,

Bring light to the city of dis,
The feelings that daylight bring,
Think stale, old, thoughts,
Looking toward the past.

Chords which are worn without,
Feeling which emotion never
Brings, the light which are
Grasp for the little things,
Which recall tomorrow's flame.

UNTITLED

You must be hammer,
or anvil

I see you know,
Your Goethe,
Number six!

I am not a number,
I am a free man!

I will not be
Pushed,
Filed,
Stamped,
Indexed,
Briefed,
De briefed,
Or numbered!
My Life Is My Own!

UNTITLED

Twisted shades of reds and blues,
Forming in my mind's dark eye,
Shape tomorrow's ghostly hues,
The future as it sighs.

Midnight's sorrow grapples fast,
Clutching thoughts and asking "why"?
Is time-lost hope all that fast
Yesterday's ever wise.

Golden dawn untangles now,
Bringing colour as I lie,
The peace that forces me to bow,
The knowledge of life's lies.

Returning through the haze
Of a lost year,
The last year,
Of a person now so changed.

The outward journey

Through madness,
Most now blessedly forgotten,
Changed and warped he who was.

A path of rocks, hurdles, spears,
Piercing the core in a
Fusion of golden guilt,
Melting the past, the ego.

Then splendid return,
A glimmering light,
A blessed darkness,
Emerging anew,
Without the scars.

HEUTE, DIE WELT - MORGEN...?

Torn and tangled,
Tried and tested,
Fey and fading,
Fast and falling,
This is the way,
The whimpering ends,
Not through the world,
But in a bang.

Subtle explosions,
Of values unfurling,
Matted heirs,
To fortunes undreamt,
Escape is impossible,
Resistance is futile,
The old cliches,
Pave the new way.

WITH AGE COMES...

Do not pass judgement,
Old one,
For your time is past.
You who cannot know,
Cannot speak,
With authority
I say this.

In days of old,
Your nights were golden,
But now your days
Are grey and empty.
Close your door,
Old one,
For your time is past.

The cold creeps forward,
Chilling your mind
To harsh, bitter spite.
We do not heed you,
Speak to your ghosts,
Cry to your memory,

Who will remember you,
Old one,
When you have passed?

Gorizia-N.E. Italy
06/04/92

THE GRASS IS GREENER

England is empty,
Grey and emotionless,
Folk without passion,
Coldly there!
Thought before action,
Always their way,
England hosted their day.

To the future I look,
To pasture greener,
A new land,
Full of a vitality,
Free from the claims,
Of man's great burden,
Free from the passionless
Civilisation.

Today may be grey,
But tomorrow shines.

Gorizia-N.E. Italy
06/04/92

OLD KRAKOW

Ancient city,
Proud and historic,
Glorious, sweeping structures,
Great and beauteous,
Gleaming,
But shadowed
In gloom and poverty.

The high walls of the castle,
Do not hide,
But rather reveal the grey,
Pall of the city's hopes.

They say that youth
Is where the hopes of
The future lie,
Hope again for the
Shining city.
But youth is here, is
Also tainted with sadness.
The only hope of the city

Is without hope.

Farewell, good city,
And good fortune.

Gorizia-N.E. Italy
06/04/92

DEVOTION

The pen may be mightier than the sword,
But nought so strong as the spoken word,
Give me the chance and you will see,
The worth of the words which I give to thee.

Gorizia-N.E. Italy
08/04/92

TOGETHERNESS

Children of the world unite,
Together we stand,
Together we fight.
The old sayings still hold true,
The world belongs to me,
And I belong to you.

Teachers teach but empty words,
Empty of meaning, empty of light,
While others follow in passive herds,
Together we stand,
Together we fight.

Remember my child the future is ours,
Everything which we see,
Your followers will fight your wars,
But you belong to me.

Gorizia-N.E. Italy
08/04/92

UNTITLED

In body and soul,
Together entwined,
Separate entities,
Sharing one mind,
One thought
One life,
One love.

Forever,
Together,
Entwined.

TIME AND (E) MOTION

Words without meaning,
Time without ending,
Living in hope
Of a new inspiration,
Working in reaches
Flung far
To the winds,
Time never ends.

Sitting in places,
Where faces are people,
Leaving the chance,
Of old recollection,
Of all of our striving,
To fate
And the winds,
Time never ends.

Music conspiring,

To bring us in the moment,
Dancing with faith
Of a short domination,
Expressing the words,
As free
As the winds,
Time never ends.

Passing from rights
That flicker and shine,
Wishing the end
Of this disintegration,
All that remains,
Is dust
In the wind
Time is at an end.

Krakow-S. Poland
28/03/92

REVELS OF BACCHUS

The sun was approaching its zenith, leeching moisture from the air, trailing in a relentless arc across the burning sky as Robert steered the Bentley up the drive and into the courtyard of his great-uncle's house. His house now, he reminded himself, although house, as a word, would be inadequate to describe the sprawling heap which lay spread before his eyes. Drawing up in front of the huge oaken door which marked the entrance to his legacy, Robert brought the car to a standstill and, having removed the keys, caressed the stylised key-fob fondly, recalling the girl who had given it to him as a token of her love on the day before he was to depart for University. A sweet young thing she was, open and honest with him in everything, little suspecting that time and Oxford life would change Robert and, with him, their relationship. The young man sighed and placed the key-fob and its burden in his pocket, Caroline really had been a rather charming young thing in her own way, not a patch on some of the girls he'd known since and terribly naive of course, but nevertheless quite charming.......

(a)   Just remember pride – too much of it...
(b)   Humility is a better one word (to remember).
(c)   Sobriety is better still...

UNTITLED

Shallow little people,
Living shallow lives,
Oblivious to all
but their devices,
They think of nothing
but themselves,
Minds like
Unbundled fires
Thought into their subconscious never delves.

"Let them be happy," he said with a smile,
Bored with his opulence great,
this holy decree without evil or guile,
His joyous form empty of hate.

His people were hungry, their familiar cried,
In their poverty tired and morose,
As he thought of them then he sat and he sighed,
Whilst enjoying propensities gross.

Chaos reigns in the land of plenty.

BEYOND

Miasmic beauty in cryptic times,
Summoned once more by one
Who rules.
Scales of beauty,
Levels of love,
The maker of lies

ABOVE

Bevelled ashlars
Stretched beyond concern
The mortal mortar ingrained
To begin, need, join,
A structure built and
Builded
To last, (at last)
Eternal

A SONG FOR EUROPE

Here, as I sit at this empty café,
Thinking of you,
I remember all those moments
Lost in wonder,
That we'll never find again.

Though the world is my oyster,
It's only a sham,
Full of memories,
And here by the Seine
Notre Dame casts a long lonely shadow.
Now only sorrow,
No tomorrow,
There's no today for us,
Nothing is there, for us to share,
But yesterday.

These cities may change,
But there always remains
My obsession,
And through silken waters
My gondola glides,

And the bridge, it sighs.
I remember all those moments,
Lost in wonder,
That we'll never find again,
There's no more time for us,
Nothing is there,
For us to share
But yesterday.

EDITIONS OF YOU

Well I'm here looking through an old picture frame,
Just waiting for a perfect view,
I hope something special will step into my life,
Another fine edition of you,
A pin-up done in shades of blue.

Sometimes you'll find a yearning for the quiet life,
The country air and all of its joys,
But that just couldn't compensate at twice the price,
For just another night with the boys,
And boys will be boys will be boys.

They say love's a gamble,
Hard to win, easy lose,
And while sun shines you'd better make hay,
So if life is your table and fate is the wheel,
Then let the chips fall where they may,
In modern times and modern ways.

And as I was drifting past the borderline,

I heard the sixty sirens wail,
So look out sailor if you hear their croon,
You'll never be the same again,
That crazy music drives you insane,
This way...

Who knows what, you muddle my brain,
So love me, leave me, do what you will,
Learn from your mistakes is my only advice,
And stay cool is still the big rule,
Don't play yourself for a fool,
Too much cheesecake too soon,
Old body's better than new,
No mention in the latest Tribune,
And don't let this happen to you.

2HB

Oh, I was moved by your screen dream,
The celluloid pictures are living,
Your death could not kill our love for you.
Take two people, romantic,
A smoky night-club situation,
Your cigarette traces a pattern.
Here's looking at you, kid,
Never forget,
Here's looking at you, kid,
At least not yet,
Your memory stays,
It lingers ever,
Fade away never.

White jacket, black tie, wings too,
You gave her away to the here,
Words don't express my meaning,
Notes could not spell out the score,
But finding, not keeping's the lesson.
Here's looking at you, kid,
Celebrated,
Here's looking at you, kid,

Wipe away the tears,
Your memory stays, it lingers ever,
Now I hope it's for ever

Fade away never.
Fade away never.

JUST ANOTHER HIGH

Maybe your heart is aching,
I wouldn't know, now would I?
Maybe your spirit's breaking up,
Well, I shouldn't care, now should I?

Maybe you're thinking of me,
Well, I don't know, now do I?
If only you knew how I feel, oh,
I wish I could die, now don't die.

And I'm just another crazy guy,
Playing at love was another high,
Just another high.

Lately it's been so empty here,
Though I suppose that's alright,
Maybe tomorrow's not so clear,
Still I remember last night,
Singing to you like this is

My only way to reach you,

And though I'm too proud to say it,
Oh, how I long to see you.

Shattered my dreams by your goodbye,
Up-scattered my hopes that filled the sky
With your love, goodbye,
I'm just another crazy guy,
Playing at love was another high,
Just another high,
I'm just another crazy guy,
Playing at love was another high,
Such a crazy high.
Just another high,
Just another high.

CAN'T LET GO

Well I rush out blazing, my pulse is racing,
As the rain streams down my face,
There's no turning back now, the fire fades,
Outnumbered and out of place,
They said go west, young man at best,
They said you'll feel no pain,
Well that's okay if you dig the grave,
But I want to live again,

Can't let go, there's a madness in my soul tonight,
Can't let go,
must I ride it like a storm?
Can't let go,
will I run out of control tonight?
Can't let go,
It's too late the rush is on.

It's a winding road the rest of the way
Down sunset to the beach,
And Canoga Park is a straight sail drive,
That's too far out of reach,

And now the headlights are flashing by so fast,
All directions seem the same,
And the windscreen wipers keep repeating the beat,
And I can't let go again,

What's in a name of the streets tonight?
I'm only a face in the crowd,
I'm all in the dark and afraid tonight,
There's nowhere to run or to hide,
And I can't let go,
No…..no…..no

Sometimes the world outside will take you in,
With just a smile,
And you're so blinded with desire,
A hundred sleepless nights have left me wasted
And so cold,
But I can take it I'm hanging on,

Can't let go,

There's a madness in my soul tonight,
Can't let go,
Must I ride it like a storm?
Can't let go,
Will I run out of control tonight?
Can't let go,
It's too late the rush is on
Can't let go, oh, no, oh, no,
I can't let go....

Lately it's been so empty here,
Though I suppose that's alright,
Maybe tomorrow's not so dear,
Still, I remember last night.
Singing to you like this is,
My only way to reach you,
And though I'm too proud to say it,
Oh, how I long to see you.

Shattered my dreams by your goodbye,

Up-scattered my hopes that filled the sky,
With your love, Goodbye,
I'm just….
Playing….
Just another….
Such a crazy high

UNTITLED

To defy the outer
Others, the cold ones
Who needed no heat.
At least if they did,
They were still cold
Inside and this inner
Cold showed in their
Eyes on the outside,
Where they were never
Meant to be,

I gazed to the west,
And, my god! There was smoke
Somebody in this
God forsaken time,
This equally forsaken
Peace, still had the
Guts to burn things
To keep warm.

Old man in an

"Omit" shirt,
Old, so old..
"A sign of the times,"
They used to say, new
Merely a sign of
Times past, an age past,
Inhabited only by the aged

ALISON

Scent and Scentability,
The sweetness of my own true sweet,
The pure taste of ecstasy, (love unbounded)
Embodied within,
Without I am lost for ever more
For your delectation,
Unwell, unfit, unwilling
Can't be bothered to attend,
Know this it matters not.
Now the moment passes,
Going wearisome paths of ease
Help yourself, everyone, or
Leave it until later on.

UNTITLED

A teasing dog,
With salivary ball
That's rather good.
Big dog,
With happy smile,
Furrily competent.

The world seen
Through another
Pair of spectacles
Is a borrowed moment,
Irreverent and blank,
Rose-tinted venom
And thoughtless desire,
Make us what we are,
And ever were crafted to be.

The hollow cries of sullen gulls,
Heralded approach of one,
Who, cyan girded, aproned nobly,
Dim his faith and truth defend
A just and upright man came forth,

Across a turbulent sea, through waters of peril
And dreams of wind,
Arrived to calm
The troubled folk.
They welcomed him
But stood aside,
Circling as beasts
In search of Prey,
Carrion for their own fulfilment,
Dead at heart,
Yet Still waiting.

Sallied not,
Our hero sallied forth,
Oblivious to hate and discontent,
With fortune sweet upon his shoulder.
Inspiring more, resolved and cheering
A constant smile, niched and lurking.

Island of the displaced,

Misplaced, misunderstood,
Misinformed, as knowledge is indeed power,
The powerless have enough to resist, subsume
And, ultimately, succeed.
Would you care to venture,
When so very few would venture to care?
It matters not…

SENIOR CITIZENS

Summer soiree,
Seeking,
Searching,
Senseless,
Even.
A summoning of the
Sickened moulted.
Laughing,
Smiling,
Disappointed.
Anything New Today...?

YOURS SINCERELY

I look in your eyes
And see wheels within wheels,
A fast fascination of depth.
I hear your voice
And feel time out of space,
A sensual siren of need.
I breathe in your perfume
And scent summer days,
A mesmerism of Warmth

A CHALLENGE

I believe in her,
In everything she does
Do my eyes deceive me?
Does my mind deceive my eyes?

As I think of the way
That she makes my life complete,
I shudder within
Is this dependency?
Like a drug she penetrates,
With needle-sharp ecstasy,
And I will not hear,
A word against her,
I feel everything.
So I believe in her,
I must. But does she, believe in me?

ITALIAN CLUBS – GOOD AND BAD

The "Ange Bleu",
or the "Blue Angel"
as we would call it
in English is a most
unfriendly place. They impose
the strictest dress codes
and do not like foreigners.
For foreigners they read
"anyone they don't like the
look of": "This Means You ."
Beware, for they take
advantage of anybody who
speaks English as a 1st language.

INSPIRATION

I once wrote a poem,
Hemingway and food,
The milk I had
Was not of Cain
Nor anything so rude
The firing squad of boredom
Watched while I stood and bled.
And not a single one of them.
Understood a word
I said.

The inner lust of purity,
Which faces the brutality
Of shameful guilt which shudders by,
The beauty
Which doth lie beside
The animus of jealousy,
The weird
Knighthood of unity
As juices flow
And powers grow
Amazing feelings start
To show

SAVE

And when the light goes out
I am bought and sold,
My mistress sees
She boils,
I serve
Her every whim,
Her every curve
My mission is to please
My purpose her life
To ease,
Her pleasure
Is in my giving
And me to receive.

WEAKNESS

Not setting fire to next door's shed,
Not making sure the other's dog is dead,
Not knocking doors to drum up Business,
Not walking out with business unfinished,
Not leaving fellows and friends bereft
Not
Not caring
When nothing is left.

LOOKING FORWARD TO SILVER (HI-HO)

Lock the door
And leave the key,
Happy anniversary,
You'll get all the things
From me
You think
But I shall disagree,
The shoe may fit
The foot you have
The bed you made
The polished smile,
A hideous brogue of weathered sheen,
Self ridicule
Of lapping tongue
The while.
And what might have, and could, have been.

You piss on snails
But where's your shell?
Consigned to yet
Another hell.

As grass grows round
Your fingertips
You realise.

KATIE'S POEM

You f..... evil b.....,
Shag your girlfriend and I'll pay,
And when she takes her teeth out,
Sans Steradent you'll rue the day.

With guns and brain, you'll venture gain,
But fortunes lost at balance cost,
The value of your broken Vow,
Is nothing,
Purgatory Now.

CLOSURE

As one opens up another goes away,
The toil of September
Is another day,
In café, writing, library,
Or schemes in founded play,
Where listening is overdue,
And naturally obey.
The feeding song of abstinence,
Frustration and desire,
The calling card of elegance
In Poesy's
Funeral Pyre.

PISS TROUGH

Silent, waters
Stagnant,
Pooling,
Coruscation added.

Swirls of clear and purifying novelty
To cause the eddy
Aid the flow
'Round Icebergs Green
And faith unseen
To dark domain
Where nature's froth remains.

NOT A GARDENING IMPLEMENT (IN THE VERNACULAR)

A trenchant sphere of ugliness,
Is yours,
Or is it in your dress?

A fatal flaw in sight for horses,
You flaunt,
As when you tread the boards

A final bow to beauty goes,
Your kiss,
The poison, Purple Pro's ...

RE-WRITE

The rubber
On the end
Of a pencil.

Erases all our memories.
As if they never were.

Joy,
Sorrow
Glee
Regret

All erased,
By the pencil's
Cruel turn.

STREAMS OF CONSCIOUSNESS, RIVERS OF THOUGHT

(Torrents of passion, floods of regret)

When the sun sets
Over the stream
Of consciousness.
Do the dying rays reflect,
On the still waters of memory?

It is not necessarily,
The Manna from heaven,
We receive that is important,
But we receive it.
The Manner in which

WHY BOTHER?

People running,
Shooting,
Touching,

Feeling nothing,

Vacant thoughts,
If there can be
Such a thing.

It is here,
Amongst the
Vicarious throng

As they hear
The song
Of others.

MUSIC

Motor head,
Petrol head,
Wait for the
Explosion
When you're
Apposite.

I'm not going
To give
The obvious
Rhyme.

I frankly
Can't be arsed
And don't have
The time

To waste
Upon my tastes.

THIS

The constant
Cacophony,
Cackle
Of sound,
The cabaret!
Old and new,
Trouble brews.
With violence,
Restrained for far,
Too long,

It will out,
As all things do,
And, as it descends,
Will take us all
Down,
With it.

PROFIT AND LOSS

A perfect couple,
Garbed
In emerald green.

Eyes to match,
Smiles to match,
With grace
As yet unseen,

Those emerald ways,
Perfect love,
Perfect life,

A true gem
In a sea
Of coal black
Darkness
Shining-emerald beauty.

DRIPPING TAPS

Our lives are all just
Dripping taps,
Leaking,

The washer,
Of consciousness.
Leaking life

As it drips away,
Drop by painful drop,
Drip by painful drip

Leeching away
Hearts,
Minds,
Souls,

Every aspect
Of humanity,
Reduced

To the drip,
Of a faulty,
Tap.

1-0 (MEDITERRANEAN SET)

Or, the tragedy,
The pain
For peninsular
People
Of the land called
Spain

Expectations turned around,
On a south-African
Football ground,

A ball in the net,
With a deadly kiss,
Tapped in by the wick man city,
Swiss.

Spain victims of complacency,
Forgetting their foes
Mostly play and train.
In Italy.

SMILE

We are none of us anything
Without a sense of humour,

If we lose all else,
When fortune fades,

Time may be the healer,
But laughter saves the day,

ASPIRATION FOR MANKIND

The curve of the beautiful breast,
As soft and tempting
As the horizon,
Offering endless possibilities,
Endless opportunities, for nurture + nature + for future
And, as the earth,
Curves and flows,
With cloud covered grace,
So might we,
With patience,
Find our hand,
Encircle that perfect breast

FEELING DOWN?

Kept down,
Count down,
Defcon 2,
For the human mind,
Melt-down imminent,
Adversaries poised,
But the words of a friend
Survive,
And keep the human mind
Alive,
So-
Back to Defcon 5.

COW - WATCHING FOR BEGINNERS

One ruminates,
When looking at cows,

Chewing the cud,
Of thoughts and feelings,

Settling our inner selves.
Into a placid place,
Where no hurt happens.

Voices heard,
In the hero,

But ultimately
Docility
Leads to making of our
Talents
Or the dinner plate.

ON FELINES

Where do the cats
Come from?

Other cats,
Obviously,

And those,
In their turn,

From previous cats

But what makes them
What they are?

Who they are?

Environment or force of will?
The latter, I think –
They mean no ill.

We're just a bit big

To serve as prey,

But big enough to serve,
Nonetheless

That will do for your
Average cat....
If such a thing there is.

After all,
For all of us,
Feline or primate.

It's difficult
To find good staff
And keep them.

RAINBOW GIRL

Red the ruby of your lips,
The treat within your tender kiss,

Orange, warmth of your embrace,
The touch of a
St. Ives sunset,
Yellow vanilla scent
Of your perfume
That lingers when you
Leave the room,

Green your eyes of emerald,
Shining gems in a perfect
Setting

Blue clarity of a cloudless sky,
Pure as your thoughts,
Intents and purpose,

Indigo dreams of your summer
Dress,
Flowing with the grace

Of your confident stride

Violet passion
Kept inside
Deep, dark and fierce,

My rainbow girl,
A spectrum,
Of perfection,

Brightening the
Dismal day,
But always out of reach.
At the other end
Of the rainbow bridge.

THE EX-RAINBOW.

Red, your eyes
Booze driven rage,

Orange
Fake tan on your visage,

Yellows, jaundiced
As our love,

Green, the envy
In your soul

Blue, cerulean
Depression in your heart,

Indigo, random behaviour
Neither one, nor the other

Violet violence,

Vitriol.
At the other end of the rainbow bridge.

Dystrophic fantasy,
Of failing feelings,
The vine
Whispers on the bough,

SELF TAUGHT (TAUT-OLOGY)

Aspirations
Perspirations,
Long drawn out
Inhalations,

Taking us to
Our destinations,
In our self-made educations

The journey to knowledge,
Not one, that can be
Learned in college,

The knowledge of oneself
And others

That we are,
One and all,
Sisters and brothers.

FISH

With some rhyme and without reason,
All is fishing out of season.
Expurgation of the soul,
Emigration of the whole,

Rake-ing in
Flake-ing out,

Cast a line,
Whiting,
Pouting,
Thoughts collide,

Memories and reason,
All the things
We keep inside

But cast a line,
There is no doubt.
We'll catch a trout,
From our streams ×3
Of consciousness.

Bet,
Without a doubt
We'll fish a trout
From our streams
Of consciousness.

HALF - EMPTY BED.

Half-empty bed,
The cool and the warm,
Sheets becalmed,

I rest my head,
In a half - empty bed,

The closeness
Becomes closure,
The ceasing becoming seizure,
I rest my head
In a half- empty bed,

And though I try,
To chat and laugh,
To fill that empty
Other half...

We know

That warmth
Is now so cold

The cooling
Of the pillow
Which once was twofold.

Now cold,
Leaving

A half-empty bed.

VOICES

Walking through the town today,
A fellow passed,
I heard him say

"Right My Lover"
Then he went,
With echoes
Of a Welsh accent,

Another chap,
Praising pasties loud,
Standing right out from the
Crowd,
Before, I'd never met this man,
But I'd swear he was from Birmingham

And then,
On a wander by the front,
A lairy Russian
Such-an impediment on an
Otherwise happy day.

And then –
My lord!
Oh, sweet surprise!

A Cornish accent
In St. Ives...

11/06/10

WHAT CALMS YOU DOWN?

The steady click of needles,
The weaving of wool?
Or thousands of feet
In a parachute fall?
Two hundred M.P.H, on a motorcycle,
Going on the straight,
The thrill,
That your skill,
Can control your fate,
Or just writing it down,
With good company,
Forget Diazepam and the rest,
- a few beers, a few words,
For me that's the best,
Then being able to share it.
Everyone can truthfully say-
"Yes, I can relax - just in my own way"
09/06/10

THE GIG RACE

Strong backs bared,
On a sun-glazed sea,

Arms tensed,
Minds geared,
Hearts apace,
Ready for the off,
Ready for the race,
The wait,
The endless wait,
Seconds as hours,
Then –
Go!

Adrenaline rush,
With salt-rimmed paddles,
The push of foot,
On sea-soaked stretchers,
The straining cords,

The growing blisters,

The acme of the heat,
The thrill of the chase

The growing panic of the
Chased,

The spray,
The spume,
The sweat of honest effort,

A mile to go,
And turn!
Dig oars! Die stroke!

Pull away bow!
Fast ten!
Hard twenty!
Blades digging deeper,
Through the briny treacle,

Feeling thicker

By the moment,

The rhythmic thud,
Of wood upon wood,
Becomes a cadence,
Burying thought

One more turn,
And race for the end,
The last reserves,
Of exhausted strength tapped,

A final desperate dash,
Jostling, jockeying,
Blades clashing,
Harsh calls and harsher feelings,
As buttocks chafe
And hands are bleeding

The finish line is

Finally crossed,

For those who won,
And those who lost,

The victors in plaudits
And praise are covered,
But all of us have truly suffered.

Never again!
(Until next time, of course).

09/06/10

FINE NIGHT OUT.

We'll have a fine night out,
On account of the fact that
It is
We'll have a fine night out,
There's nothing there to.
Spoil it for us.
We'll have a fine night out,
And everything'll be grand,
We'll have a fine night out,
I'm telling you – understand?
We'll have a fine night out,
And go to a place I know,
We'll have a fine night out,
Only don't talk unless I say so.

We'll have a fine night out
A happy time, with fun,
We'll have a fine night out,
You're safe with me, I have....
And anyway, when we get
Home, the first thing that
You'll say.

Is that we've had a fine night out,
The evening was swell,
Won't you?
Well?

Write or wrong?
We do what we do,
I'd rather write wrong,
Than ever wrong you.
Right?
Linguistically fascinating–
How Are You →
How're Ya →
HiYa →
Hi – ?

UNTITLED

Desperate, distant, factored
Fragments of personality.
A confluence emerges,
Convergence of souls
Lost, broken, and ultimately
Self regenerative.
The end result
Remains to be seen.

INSIGHT:
Absence does make the
Heart grow fonder.

OVERHEARD CONVERSATION AT DAN LOWRY'S

TAVERN, CORK. (A.K.A. THESPS...)

The warmth of mellow conversation,
Easy times with company,
The flow of life with thoughts
So carefree,
Languor beckons dreamily.

Lethargy and understanding,
Soon become the same design,
The flow of life once so
Demanding,
Happily is left behind.

Bitter streams of pale
Reflection,
Wooden grains of painful
Hue,
Star struck founts with
Dim correction,
Sounding fire with wrought

Dispute.

Arse in hand with cap
Unbended,
Doffing only pleasantry,
Motors run with tiresome
Gentry,
Lofty words from peasantry.

ALISON

Head locked,
Dead locked,
Trapped in holy wedlock

Enmity,
Ferocity,
Blatant animosity

Bitching,
Sniping
Constant undermining,
Too late,
Oh, so cruel of fate to find,
That two who were once of one mind,
To be together, forever entwined,
Were never really the marrying kind.

GIBBONS

Colour surrounds the fall of Empires,
The purples, crimson leaping,
The golds and silvers, green,
Marble white a sullied grey.

Sound envelopes Empire's death,
Laughter into cries,
The shrieks of pleasure now of pain,
Commands born of arrogance whimpers of terror

Stench overwhelms Empire's glory,
The rich perfume of decay,
Exotic spice to mouldering must,
That one sweet smell now bitter.

As our empire falls,
Its magnificence, crumbling
Its splendour, tarnished,
It's life expiring,
Born anew in a parody
Of its part.

THE GREAT VILE SHIFT

In the darkness I travel,
Ever descending.
The destination is unknown,
My own personal gear simply drives

An eternal descent looms,
Vastly downward,
whilst anticipation of an ending
Beckons becomingly
Striving with the knowledge,
That such cannot be.

Questioning the Fates,
I attempt to change my path,
Vainly striving.
Yet the knowledge which

Overcomes all reason
Dictates that nothing can ever Change.

Everlasting perdition

In the inescapable goal,
Consciously avoided, Yet,
Constantly pursued.
To conclusion,
I cannot imagine
Or rather avoid,
Though in so doing
Ultimately, I who follow
Will in turn be followed
By others unwilling

ARTIST'S PORTRAIT OF A YOUNG MAN

Contrived, the faces that look,
Contrived, the voices which smile,
Contrived, the feelings which surge,
All contrived, the inner turmoil –

Of will,
The lead becoming the
Blithely pushing,
In a bleakly drawn loop
Which elaborately coils,
To entrap and re-unite the one.

DECK OF CARDS

Tartan trousers
Grimly lashing
Open bodies
Dimly searching

Bleach-blonde hair,
Lively dancing,
Proudly touched,
Vainly prancing.

Darkened garments,
Sullen mooded,
Introverted,
Ever loaded,

Individuality,
In grouped
In suit.

AUTUMNAL EDEN

The haze of early morning,
Observes the four facades,
As light peers dimly,
Enchanting
Beckoning with coy, cold, beans,
The leaves shimmering in
Indolent breeze
The post-rimmed pathways
Of mulch –lined gravel
Surrender to the tread of feet
While gnomish pushes loiter
Guarding their secrets with
Idle Charm
The greens, the browns, the sparkling russets
This is morning,
This is the garden,
This is life.

UNTITLED

The tempestuous flow of
Your thoughts through my mind.
The pummelling beat of your heart,

Sings to my soul in a
Sinuous cry
The beauty of life,
Without hope.

Muttering doubt intervenes
With no mercy,
Shimmering visions intrude,
The memories press ever
Deeper, with laughter,
In an ecstasy
Of despair.

UNTITLED

Welcome to your home
From home,
Be unhappy here as well.

The natives are friendly,
A family, surrogate,
Equally strange and remote.

Accommodation comprises
Familiar comforts,
It should be simple enough
To spend your nights in
Sleepless turmoil,
Restlessly reassuring.

Sparkling patterns of
Shimmering light,
Moving in liquid joy,
Unbridled passions of
Strength, flowing bright,
The wonder of nature,
Delighted, aglow.

The loneliness of the
Long distance rower,
Six men in a boat with
Expressions of joyous agony,
Tearing, wrenching pleasure,
The triumph of the will.
Elemental struggle,
The sea doesn't mind,
The rest doesn't matter
Only the race remains,
Primeval but mostly human.

£39,95(O!)

A spacious detached
Residence, set in its own
Grounds in a picturesque
Rural environment.
Accommodation briefly comprises:
Entrance vestibule which
In turn provides access to
The main living area which
Is open plan, incorporating
A sitting / sleeping area.
Bathroom facilities are situated
In a nearby block, with
Convenient al-fresco dining
Area
Outside the gardens are mainly
Laid to lawn and afford splendid
Views incorporating woodland,
Countryside and glimpses of the sea.

UNTITLED

Insanity prevails,
The efforts of mankind,
Create only what
The lunatic may find

Dismal and creeping,
The spirit of life,
As the mistress is pleasure
But money the wife.

Poor and pathetic,
The dignity lost,
Ours the power,
The glory,

What of the cost ...

UNTITLED

Dark when I awake each day,
The silence echoes out,
The world sleeps on,
I seek escape,
The dim and dreary walls
Laugh back .
I race through reason,
Tear through storms,
The walls surround my
Hopes and dreams,
A life and love collide
In treason.
Doors are closed on
Nascent screams
Weeping sores of mental
Anguish,
Radiate from tortured
Realms.

Feeling dies in
Paradoxical
Here all begins,
And all must end.

UNTITLED

The sunlight dapples on
Wind blown gold,
A smile as bright as ice,
Wavering swells diminish
Not the depth of
Inspiration,
Nor the muse.

A fleeting glance,
A perfect touch,
A hastily spoken word,
A stolen kiss,
A look reduced,
A murmur,
Never heard.

A flaxen wing
Of tenderness,
Tightly stretched in line,
Founding waters,
Glimmering,
Perfection,
Re-designed.

UNTITLED

A time for profit,
A time for peace,
A time for conflict,
Of sadness,
Of loss.
Time enough to marvel
In the silent murk
Of life's own contradictions

A creeping canker of
Little acts,
Plied by little actors,
Upon little stages,
The great and the grand,
Forcefully sidle
Into the half-shadows
Of one's own half life.

All the world's a rage,
And those of us who play
Are simply stayers,
Our waves may scan

In uncertain parody,
The dusk and dismal
Night,
Of misbegotten delight

UNTITLED

Still and silent stations,
Stirring not,
The waves of foam,
Where movement is forgot,
The passive movement,
Anchored on the tide,
Bow and stern both rigid,
With their rise,
The grey of menace,
Beauty held within,
The camouflage of mirth,
The final joke,
Original sin.

SEAMUS

On a pavement in St. Giles,

a drunken man's promise

of anarchy,

and poetries,

your books I'd read,

and went to hear

and see your commentaries,

but of your's you would

not reprise

a young man setting

for,

a reason now not knows,

and yet, forever,

fears,

he denies.

UNTITLED

What is the poet?
The trolley of gold
And green,

The carrier of old
And new,

Supporter of smoke
In light-limned shadow.

He is it,
She is you,

We are all.

Beloved.

UNTITLED

Paradise ,
Bliss,
Awakened by the Siren's kiss,
Turmoil and trauma,
Fade away,
Trite expositions

A sandy place
A dust-blown wasteland
A hopeful pyramid of knowledge
A retreat.
Doom and glory,
Faith and despair,
Joy and cynicism,
"isms" all fall
Down.
A blaze of
Gory
Story
Telling
Secrets
Never to be

Sold. - Subject to contract.

Chanticleer dances while the
Ferocity of chained Katrina keeps
Busy, with a winning smile

The beauty of the dance
With practised innocence.
All the world's a contradiction
With terms,
Lo-term-in-ably

Stanza number five,
Pretensions of genius,
Heathen fires
Of man-made shells,
Revolving through rifled pasts
Toward endless personal
Hells.

UNTITLED

The beast is back ,
Is back,

Double ration
The shame of a nation,

Rindless , grindless,
Mindless, scheming.

Who will win? Who will lose?
Who really cares?

As long as we
Are still in place .

After all,
We're only

Making
Bacon.

UNTITLED

The braille imprint of past
Impressions gives the flavour
    Of the moment

Times to come as time ticks slowly,
Counting counters flipped by children.
Random thoughts fly,
Gently beating drums of toyness
With wings which under angels sigh.

Thrice blessed the man who sees
Through delirious eyes
    Of prophecy

PORTRAIT OF THE ARTIST

AS A VULTURE -

Or a Voltaire?
Velociraptor?
Virgin territory,
Vapid
Vitriolic
Vacant vicissitude.
Valiant
Venal
Victorious
Vindicated
And ultimately sin -
Dictated

KATRINA

Sweet Katrina,
Whose tempestuous kiss,
May drown the dreams of man,
Yet kindle the fires of love,
With emerald eyes that swim,
Amid swirling clouds of others' gloom,
Your graceful walk, with passing eddies,
Causing ripples in your wake.

Admired from afar,
Feared when approaching,
Longed for at distance
Observers eyes waiting
As desperation calls
Redemption waits in your sweet arms

FREYJA

Sweet Freyja,
My Nordic goddess,
Mother of light,
And love.

Your glacial beauty,
Inspires the soul,
Brings forth these
Humble scribbles,
Which cannot do
Sweet justice
To you

UNTITLED

Why the hell not?
After all,
It's only a game.

Isn't that what they
Always say
Just before they take
The dice

Away.

UNTITLED

The piss-fouled basin of man's
Desire,

Basic urges thrust to inspire
A tangent panegyric of gilt gift layered

With musical groans,

The panegyric.

SPOT THE DON - A PROLOGUE

The more things change, the more they stay
The same, so the saying goes.
I am sat, day 2, SAT. (abbrev.) (appropriate English)
In the Lamb and Flag, where my name adorns a Trophy which, by observation, is no longer Displayed. Past glories forgotten?
No.
Gone but not forgotten.
Anyway, a stone's throw from St. John's
The college wherein I gained my glory
And disgrace. I am doing now what I
Did then – to whit, sitting, drinking,
Smoking and wittering, not, as I should
Have, attending, writing or exercising
Myself in any of the scholarly pursuits
Which my previous attainments has earned
Me
Dilettante?
For certain. Living the dream, or, at
Least, up to it. To the fullest .
I sit here. Smoking, drinking, wittering, delaying

Playing the moment when I must walk through that gate.
That gate again.
Oh, heady youth,
Whose fires are kindled
With imagination,
How many palaces were built?
How many visions young?
What hopes and plans designed,
Only to be crushed by the fear
And guilt that maturity breeds?

Look to this
Thy final hour.
Despair not, But rather be glad
Look to this
"Look to this,
Thy alternate fate,
And do not flee destiny,
But rather embrace.

Look to this,
Thy last day,
Rejoice in mortality,
The great experience,

The great unknown.

UNTITLED

Once she was young,
Free to run and play,
At ease with herself,
At one with the world,
As are with nature.

Once she was young,
Full of hopes and dreams,
Carefree and blithe,

A smoke-filled room,
Brings thought,
And inspiration,
Drifting,
Through stale air.

Fresh ideas,
Swirl and smile,
With new inspirations,
Drifting,
Into open minds.

A rebirth from
A shrouded shell,
In Ashen spell,
Which drops, falls,
Cascades to Bright fire,
The molten heart,
Ever concealed,
Never revealed,
The burning heart,
To be healed.

SPOT THE DOG III

AFTER ALL, WHY NOT?

Journey begins with visit to
Parents' house – they are away
And somebody needs to keep an Eye.

This double spacing can't
Continue. Not enough paper and
Too much to write.

Anyway - arrive at Elburton
(I'm not supposed to go near work.
being on holiday and all) to find
blue rover (car, not dog) parked
on parents' drive.

Naturally, park straight across.
his bows and heave-ho into
the Beloveds' abode.
All seems well and I cannot
resist the temptation to re-patriate
a few choice items of literature

from the bookshelves in my old
room. Also the Edwyn Collins
CD. my mother appears to have
appropriated - will make for
good listening on forthcoming
track.

On exit, one cat, caterwauling
Hence the name, I suppose.
Cats, that is, although it was
sat on a wall.
Score so far: One Cat, One C.D,
some books, no dogs.

The obvious course of action
is to head for the South Hams
where dogs abound.
Plenty of fields, you see.
(and nearest destination)
The logical courteous Brixton-
not the one with the riots.
Although, I have been told, it
can get pretty wild on Tuesday
with Ladies cribbage Evening
at the Foxhound. Ah! The Foxhound! A Dog!

Shortcut through Penny's Lane
and at the end, at the
Junction, a huge mall of
traffic. So I can't exit the
Junction - is this peculiar time
of day particularly popular?
It's not School Run time,
unless they're letting them out
earlier and earlier these days
Couldn't blame them, mind
you - a teacher's job is
hard enough without having
to deal with children.
Suddenly the traffic flow
clears - a hiatus - like a
waterfall frozen between drops
with a magical gap between
droplets.
I see the gap and, magically
or otherwise, fill it.
I then arrive at the very
un - magical cork in the dam
of traffic- Temporary Traffic Lights ...
own these lights and

cork them too!
Traffic flow once resumed,
The procession flows towards Brixton.
As the convoy enters the village,
an elderly lady with a dog
is taking a leisurely stroll.
I think it might be a Terrier
of some description.
The dog, not the elderly lady.
Although the resemblance is
remarkable .
A flash of white hair and,
she's gone, they both are.

I'm assuming the dog was female-
she had white hair anyway.

THOUGHT ...

Do dogs look like their
Owners, or do they (the owners) become
Like their dogs?

If that is the case, then
mine shall wear a hat.

Oh, I didn't mention —
I am wearing a hat
Sunglasses too – a gift from
the Gypsies. The hat, that
is, not the shades.

Ironic, really.
The hat is meant to keep you
cool. The shades are supposed
to look cool. But at the
end of the day, all this
ensemble does it make you look
like a complete and utter arse!

The Curse Of The Gypsies!!
Knew I should have bought
That Heather.

BUCKFASTLEIGH - QUIET QUAINT,

3 pubs – All closed.
Various interesting shops, with various
interesting opening hours - none of
which appear to coincide with my visit.
The only pub that is open is a
"Time warp" visitor centre / museum,
3 Quid a throw and it doesn't
sell beer,
Have covered approx., 3 miles on foot
looking for Masonic Hall, only to
discover I parked ten yards
from it.
Back in the car and onwards
To…

P.S. Dogs — Very cute
Small old terrier
Faithful Dog waiting outside only
shop open.

ASHBURTON

ASHBURTON - A Little livelier,
with a lovely looking old
bookshop - closed.
99p for a Harry Potter hero!
Hurrah!

Found a pub open! Victoria Inn,
complete with beams and horse brasses.
Had pint and left as the clock chimed.

On way back popped into the "Bay horse"
which I'm beginning to suspect
should be the "Gay horse" - clientele
- Me, 2 strange gentlemen, one drinking
straight (?) tomato juice, the other
ginger beer (Rhyming slang?).
The Barman looks like a murderer–
to enforce the impression, he has got
some songs on the Jukebox
(1) Who wants to live forever
(2) Take my breath away
(3) Too much love will tell you.

Conclusion - Gay Strangler - think I'll move on ...

Have only seen 2 dogs in
Ashburton - one guide dog, one
made of stone in a garden
ornament shop- The ornament
looked happier, even though it
was asleep

I have long suspected that
wheelie- bins were the Devil's work,
and Ashburton has confirmed it
They are black. This implies
A number of things, but foremost
in my mind is this: Mondays,
Wednesdays and Fridays —
Wednesday - Brown Bin - Kitchen Waste
Friday - Green Bin - Recyclables
Monday (today) - Black Bin- Sacrificial Victims.
Glad I wasn't here last night
Royal Oak- doesn't sell Stella, but
reassuringly expensive at €2.50 a pint
nevertheless. Clientele exists-obviously
local and friendly. Courteous bar staff -

seems a shame to leave, but ...

Dog number 3 !
Smiley Collie, no lead but
following his mum. Bless.

YEALMPTON

Thought I saw
Simon's car parked outside
"The Volunteer" so had to pop in
to check. Swift half, but wish
I'd bought a space suit, as
I'm sure there's more atmosphere
on the Moon.
Perhaps there are other customers—
they must have seen me coming
and hidden behind the pool table.
Just checked – nope – this place
really is deserted, even the
barmaid has disappeared.
I'd make my excuses and leave,
but there's no-one to make them
to, so I think I'll just leave….
No Dogs At All!

ORESTON

ORESTON - Back home to
Sanity and reason, or so I think...
Weird things are occurring at
the Kings Arms - a party is going
on. No special occasion, no
balloons, but more life in the
place than on most nights.
Dancing about with pool cues is
a bit different for a Monday lunchtime
so why not?
One stick-fight later it is
revealed that budding computer wiz
Nikki has handed in notice at the pub
and is loving every minute of it.
Vanessa is also leaving and despite
the fact that neither are rodents,
I have the same feeling as the
Captain of the Titanic - post Iceberg ...
The atmosphere is, nevertheless, still warm.
Abba on Jukebox - have ruined people's!
lives by suggesting the words
to a particular song actually

say "Chicken Tikka" Much amusement
Ongoing.
By the way, the pub shut almost
half an hour ago and I'm still in
it, which can't be a bad thing.
Spice Girls on Jukebox now, which
can be.
Confused B.T. ... engineer, complete
with stepladder wandering from
place to place without actually doing
anything. He has a beard though,
which must count for something.
Shaky barmaid smoking a tampon
made of plastic. Nicotine substitute apparently.
Still no dogs,
Off home now...

TUESDAY

Harry Potter™ pen at the ready once more to record the magical events of this special day.
Woke rather early – no early it was still Monday, so, after brief 4 hour mooch about, went back to bed and to sleep- eventually, and not without distraction.
Waking later - approx. Ten, - discovered that it is indeed Tuesday and promptly went back to sleep.
Cup of cold tea stuck to bedside unit - not a table, not really a set of drawers anymore, but indisputably a unit with drawers. Alison removes and brings a fresh one - tea that is. The unit remains with drawers.
I find this next bit difficult. I don't like hospitals and nobody else around me seems to either - especially the people who work there, which is a little disconcerting to say the least.

After chain-smoking 3 cigarettes in as many minutes, courage is plucked up and in we go - at least the nurses do - I'm still outside, looking lost, Lost right outside the main entrance ... Alison has gone in so, I must follow - wouldn't do to go to pieces now. Make a poorly (no pun intended) considered joke about the convenience of a "Body Shop" in a hospital and then it's off to reception through a labyrinth of (hopefully) sterilized corridors. The guy at the desk admits that he can't read, which is comforting we are then sent to...WAITING AREA 8 ...

Small, but uncomfortable, with various porters pre-empting fights "If it looks like someone is Jumping the queue, please don't butt them, because they aren't really honest- Besides we have enough bloodshed to deal with already, and

you wouldn't BELIEVE the queues at
A+E!"
Dry mouthed and nervous-we've
been psyching ourselves up for this
Ali and I sit-before the lure
of the free water dispenser overcomes
all. It must be a trap and I
refuse a second cup in the nick
of time. No-one else is drinking.
They must know something.
They do.
In walks the Specialist, and calls
Alison's name.

Immediately, the small elderly gent
with the crutches struggles to his
feet, a big smile on his face.
Simultaneously, we stand, as the
Specialist frowns at him and says
"NO, AL-I-SON ...MRS."
Rather sheepishly he sits back down
and tells us he is called Alan. It
is evident he has been waiting for
a while, with a rather imposing

lady who may be his daughter.
Or his minder.
We laugh off the confusion and
I pray that they have read and
noted the sign and we won't
be attacked by Amazonian protectoresses
enraged by queue jumpers.
As it happens, we have jumped the
Queue by about a week,
Well, it's not what you know, it's
who you know, isn't it ?

In this particular instance, the
Consultant who arranged the appointment
doesn't appear to know his arse from
his elbow, but does seem to know
whoever books in the tests.
He must like Alison – he's got her
in a week before it's ever safe
to do so. Private healthcare
eat your heart out - or get somebody
(no pun intended) to do it for you,
after all that's why it's not free.
This is revealed by a rather stern,

though competent looking, lady who
announces herself as Doctor Pearson,
turns on her heel and marches up the
corridor with the words -
"Follow me. I saw you drinking
water. This test should be conducted
with an empty bladder. Never mind,
come on."
As the door is closed in my face
Dr. Pearson finally notices me and
with a pleasant ladylike snarl of
disdain , growls - "There's a seat over
there for you."
Meekly I sit.
Someone, somewhere, has made a
cock-up and the appointment is
re arranged, for, as previously stated
we are a week early and the Specialist
refuses to carry out the test. It would be
potentially dangerous to Alison and the baby
but I can't help feeling that she
would gladly try it on me - if only
to rent her anger and frustration, or

simply to experiment on a lower form of life.
As we leave, she apologies profusely to Alison and I thank her for her time.
She acknowledges with a grunt and a sneer, a dismissive, yet speculative look in her eye._
– DOGS - 0 SPROGS - 1. Full heart empty bladder...

ST. AUBYN - WARM WELCOME.

Wrong Venue ...
Arrived with plenty of time and saw
many familiar faces.
Slight feeling of unease as, having
signed in, Wardens in tow, it is
noted that this is St. Aubyn 954, not
Methan 1205 and the official visit
is from Fortitude 105-not Tamar 4239.
Nevertheless, we go to the Bar, where
Chris (J.W.) gets the beers in.
Father (S.W.), suddenly comes
running across.
"We are well and truly in the shit."
We are indeed. Thinking that we are
at an official visit held at St. Aubyn,
it turns out that we should be at
Mt. Edgcumbe Hall on the Hoe, which
explains the absence of everyone else from
Tamar whom we expected to see.
Apart from Charlie, of course.

Lulled into a false sense of security

apparently he visits St. Aubyn 954 every month…
18:35, and we dash out, drinks unfinished, bemusing the St. Aubyn welcoming party at the door.
Have we been offended? No. Simply made ourselves a laughing stock.
Never mind - pressure's on now, with only ten minutes to get to.

MOUNT EDGCUMBE MASONIC HALL —

Hah! Nick of time!
You know, it's weird really? As I was walking into St. Aubyn twenty minutes ago I felt relaxed and thought to myself how unusual this was, usually having to rush from work. Now I'm stressed again, which feels much more familiar and consequently more comforting and comfortable.

The Brethren of Tamar 4239 are arranged – finally silenced - and in we process.
I am led to the W.M., John Kingdom, who informs me that he's glad to see me and looks forward to my speech.
So that's me stitched.
Again-
Thanks, John.
Excellent ritual and decent meal, both of which were mentioned before

I got up to speak.
Said it all anyway, which seemed to
go down quite well , even though
I have the feeling that I rambled on
a bit too long. Looking forward to John's
speech or Methan's return visit...
Heh, Heh Heh
NO DOGS, BUT CLEANED UP ON THE RAFFLE

WED. KING'S ARMS, ORESTON–

Not really sure why I've called
in, but it beats being not alone at
home.
Instead, I'm sat alone here.
Completely alone.
Even Mary has disappeared off somewhere -
perhaps she's disconcerted about me
sitting here writing and just doesn't
have the nerve to ask what exactly it
is that I am writing anyway. And why
Just as well, really.
Mary has returned - apparently the
Post office will be turning up for
lunch in a minute.
"All of it" I ask, and Mary smiles
Perhaps that's a yes..
If so, that would explain our
deliveries
Mr. Bickford has a lot to answer for.
at least according to British Gas,

Human - - - B.G. - My former employer

where former office is now occupied by
the Post office ...
A connection? A conspiracy?
Perhaps they're trying to tell me something ...
At least they're not trying to sell me something.
Mary returns once more - apologised
that she can't keep me company, so
I mention that I might put a few
tunes on the jukebox. She asks if
I would rather have lockets?
Fairly witty, so my reply has to be that
I prefer Halls Soothers. It is, and I
wonder whose benefit that is actually
for.
Karen has come out of the kitchen,
knowing that I am recording things and
denying all knowledge of Monday
I promise that she has not been mentioned
by name, So that's all right, then.
Oops ....

"California Dreaming - Water Ad. Stylish

She's not there" missing Ali. She's not here.
"House of the Rising Sun"- It's been the ruin - opposite
changed these lyrics a few times.

Feeling of sixties beatnik …
Then suddenly—
"Don't You Forget About Me" -
Breakfast Club, Shenefast club - on to the
eighties with a reassuringly martial
beat. Vanity - Insecurity? The 80's
had it and still have, twenty years
down the line.
Nostalgia - It's not what it used to be …
"Golden Brown" – Best song in the world, ever.
Never a frown and every time just like the last.

Definitely the Best Song Ever!
Still no dogs, though…

Think I'd better go home and
get ready for the return to the
district of evil – looks to be a good
night …

Stuck in a continuing Hurd -
e.g. DOGLESS

Trust me – it's all in the pronunciation,

Left it a bit late, but now about to
bathe and set off for ...

BUCKFASTLEIGH –

Again- Scouting mission has paid off,
as I've parked in almost exactly the
same spot as Monday, with 18 minutes
to spare. Try to phone Alison to
smugly prove that I've done it. All
on my own, and properly dressed.
Full D.J. – Kitted out and looking good.
Ali's work line is engaged – busy girl –
but I've plenty of time, so stand
outside the previously scouted building
and enjoy a leisurely cigarette, whilst
trying to phone again- Still engaged,
so leave a message on the mobile instead.
18 minutes part four - 12 minutes to spare
so I stroll inside.
Empty....
Shit ..
Not quite totally empty, as a kindly lady
pops up from a counter and offers me
a cup of tea. —

So who's late then?" she asks.

"Not me – I'm a bit early, I think,
ten minutes at least, I must be .. "
"No, no. They Tyled at 3.30, so you're
late - very late. You may as well have
that cup of tea – you've plenty of time."
Yes – I have plenty of time ...
Not so smug now, oh?
No.
The "ordinary" Brethren come down and
commence with the relaxed banter
which they so enjoy and I quite miss
during Installations these days. I casually
ask who is here from province. —
"Oh – Robin and a few others," comes
the equally casual reply.
Shit. P.G. M. .. And "a few others" ...
How the Hell am I going to get out of
this one..?
I am the reigning Worshipful Master of
Tamar 4239 and I am also very, very late.

Signed in now. Looking at the other
names on the list, I can see that
not only am I in the shit, but I am

also going to have the piss taken out
of me in a special way, by experienced
Masters of the craft – Past Masters are better
at it and they'll have a go too.
How the Hell ...?

BLAGGED IT !
They were one short for E.A's, so I
volunteered to join the end of the
queue. I sense a theme.
The Tyler was rather annoyed that one
of the Brethren he was briefing on how
to go in had his back turned and
was instead studying a photo.
It was me.
I turned around, as one of the Brethren
Said – "Yes – he's number seven."

The P.G.M. – Robin to his friends
Got away with it, it would seem.
Still can't spell that word, wonder why.
Anyway, Robin – Okay, the P.G.M.
approaches me and consoles me for

being held up at work-hence my
delay.
Don't have the heart or the guts
to correct him, so simply agree.
He nods and smiles and I
appear to have acquired Brownie
Points simply by being late.
Should try that more often ....
A small victory as I find my name
on the seating plan - I am CIO.
As we are called to take our places
I am moved, Relocated. Re-positioned.
I am still CIO – or at least the
slip of paper says so – but I am,
in reality, B3!
Still on a spur - but right at the
Top!
Splendid company at Festive Board!
Len May on my left and Mike Tobin
almost opposite. Surprisingly didn't
take the piss.
Too Much.

Other Worshipful Brethren to my right
and opposite – nice fellows, though
one a little strange.
Shan't say which, Just in case.
One never knows, after all does one?

Have been called by name –
"Richard – Give Len May a prod will you?"
– It's the PGM speaking. Or should I
say Robin, now that he himself has
crossed the boundaries of familiarity ..?
"Yes, Sir," I reply, with all the
familiarity of a student to his
teacher (which is quite appropriate when
you think about it) and duly
prod Len May.

SPOT THE SPROG (DOG II THE SEQUEL)

WEDNESDAY, Wrote Mr. Kipling. Possibly the last thing he wrote, as I have just read the sad news of his passing. Well, not Kipling himself, but his voice. Passing on to another actor, no doubt, may he Bake well and avoid crusty tarts.

9:30 a.m. – Call to say Alison has been sent to Derriford – I immediately rush up in pursuit, Immediately after re-entering the office and sitting at my desk and trying, unsuccessfully to continue with the business of the day. The girls, bless 'em, have intimated that if I don't rush up in pursuit, then my life will not be worth living.

They will make sure of it...

Secretly relieved I embark on a sedate relaxed drive to Derriford Hospital, a distance of approximately 7-8 miles, through traffic.

I sedately arrive, in a relaxed manner, approximately 7-8 minutes later.

Alison has only just reached the car park herself and is on the mobile guiding me in.

I manage to park right behind her car, next to the parking meter and, job successfully done so far, casually saunter towards said ticket-producing device.

£ 1.40 for 4 hours, £2.00 until 8 pm.

Ever the optimist, I opt for the £2 ticket and, nervously perspiring, reach into my pocket.

No change.

At all.

Bugger.

Bugger, Bugger, Bugger, I cry, as I stamp my feet and flop my arms like a frustrated infant penguin.

I am reliably informed that penguins say these things in times of stress, but only when young, and eventually graduate to "Arse", when they reach the age of maturity.

Deciding to risk it, I walk towards Alison, saying "No change, I'll risk it." She is, perhaps, thinking that I refer to the state and availability of my underwear, and/or replacements, so I feel the need to explain. "How much for a parking ticket here?" I ask. "I've decided to risk it."

"£2.00 until 8 pm," she replies.

"Right, Okay – Fine. As in Parking."

"Oh … you might get some change Inside."

She's caught on, so we head towards the Maternity Building.

It is situated to the side of the main hospital building, shorter and, apparently just opened.

Apposite – as an off-shoot of, as it now appears, offspring, of the complex edifice towering above.

As we approach, I wonder whether this is to protect the newly-born from the other denizens of the main building, or is it the other way around … ?

ALEXANDRA

Arms wide open.
Perfect smile.
Eyes of shining
China blue
Sea green,
Peach white glow
On your complexion
You are my beloved
Dandy-Lou.

Forever smiling,
Dancing,
Singing,
Laughing..

Bringing joy,
To yourself

And the world
At large
But still, so small....

IDLE POESY

Oh, miracle of verse
That frees the soul.
From the shackles of the day.
Your words express
All that cannot be
Spoken or gestured
Simply felt.

Harmony of faith in feeling,
Sets the soul aflame
In rapturous marvel,
Kindling, the heart
That was destined to burn
With the fires
Of idle poesy.

Gorizia-N.E. Italy
06/04/92

www.ingramcontent.com/pod-product-compliance
Lightning Source LLC
Chambersburg PA
CBHW052025070526
44584CB00016B/1905